A JUNIOR ELF® BOOK

A JUNIOR ELF® BOOK

My First Book of
CARS and TRUCKS

By Diane Namm

Illustrated by June Goldsborough

CHECKERBOARD PRESS • NEW YORK

Copyright © 1987 Checkerboard Press, a division of Macmillan, Inc.
All rights reserved. Printed in U.S.A.
CHECKERBOARD PRESS, JUNIOR ELF, and their respective logos
are trademarks of Macmillan, Inc.

Once upon a time there were two magpies. Mike and Spike were their names, and they were as different as two magpies could be.

Mike flew slow and straight
ahead. Spike flew fast, racing here
and landing there.

When it came time to fly south for the winter, Spike said to Mike, "I bet I can get down south before you can!"

To which Mike replied, "Well, you can try!"
And the race was on.

Mike soared straight up into the
sky. "Slow and steady is how I'll
fly," he said.

First Spike flew circles around Mike. But after awhile, Spike thought to himself, "Perhaps I'll take a rest. I'll have no trouble catching up with him."

So Spike landed, and suddenly
he heard a VROOM, VROOM,
VROOM. Then something below
him began to move.

"That's it!" Spike cried. "I've got a plan! I'll beat old slow and steady Mike. I'll just ride on this car."

But after awhile the driver stopped. And he shooed Spike off his hood.

So Spike flew around and around, looking for another way to get down south!

Before too long, he saw a yellow taxicab. Spike flew beside the window and asked, "Can you give me a ride?"

"Sure," said the cab driver. "Just hop inside."

Soon the cabbie stopped to take a passenger for a ride. But the passenger would not get in while Spike was still inside. So the cabbie shooed Spike away.

"I've got to find another ride," said Spike as he looked up. And sure enough, there was Mike, flying slowly and steadily above.

A fire engine clattered by, hurrying down the street. "That's it!" Spike cried. "I'll hop on that, and I'll be sitting in the sun in no time flat."

But the fire engine was on its
way to put out a very big fire.
And the firemen had no time to play,
so they shooed Spike off right away.

"Now I'll have to find *another*
ride," sighed Spike. Then he looked
up. And sure enough, there was
Mike, flying steadily above.

Just then Spike saw a freight train carrying a load of grain. "That's it!" he cried. "I'll take that train south and lunch on grain at the same time."

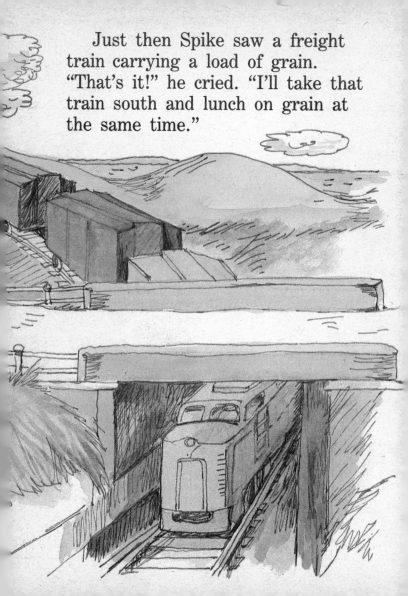

But the engineer who drove the
train did not want Spike to eat his
grain. So he, too, shooed Spike
away.

Then Spike looked up. But he did not see Mike. "I'll bet he's far behind," chuckled Spike. "And since I'm so far ahead of Mike, I think I'll stop for lunch."

Just then Spike saw a police car whizzing by. "Hmmm," he thought. "That police car is exactly what I need."

But the police officer in the car
simply did not agree.

Now Spike was really tired—
he'd had a busy day. And since
steady old Mike was nowhere in
sight, Spike found just the place to
take his nap—in a big pile of hay.

Well, that hay was heaped right on the back of a big hay truck, which just happened to be heading south.

"I made it, I won," Spike started to crow.

"What took you so long?" Mike wanted to know.

"What's that? Why how did you get here ahead of me?" cried Spike.

"I just flew the whole way, how else?" asked Mike.